MW01286753

Printed in the United States of America

ISBN 9781494870522

Dedicated to your spirit.

Acknowledgements

I would like to thank my parents Stan and DeVelma Coleman, my siblings, and the rest of my family and friends for their continued love, support, and guidance.

I also extend my admiration and appreciation to Makalia Francis-Coleman and Jeremy Moore for editing every draft of this book.

Most of all, I thank God for the gift of life.

INTRODUCTION

Each year automobile companies release new vehicles to the world with new designs, different body-styles, upgraded amenities, and much more. The same goes for brand name shoes, clothing, phones, electronics, or any other product within a company that desires to remain relevant. With a combination of technology continuing to advance and creativity continuing to pervade the human mind, the world is incessantly offered a new product or *the next best thing*. Would you agree that improvements have been made to the instruments in the field of medicine too? How about science or architecture? What about aviation, aerospace, energy, or electronics? I would postulate that your answer is yes to most of these questions, if not all. However, the real question is *why are we as people more apt to improving the things outside of us than within us*? Or to take it a step further; *why do we desire to <u>have</u> the improved product but not <u>be</u> the improved product*?

With the use of innovative quotes/philosophies, and therapeutic boxing quotes/philosophies, *IT* provides a new and *improved way of thinking* that will expand your PerspectVe™ concerning different areas of life. While paying homage to famous quotes from Les Brown, Gandhi, Helen Keller, Mark Twain, Bruce Lee and many more, this book builds on philosophies of the past and present and positions to be the next generation of quotes and philosophies in its own right.

Though there is no specificity regarding the enumeration or grouping of these quotes, the reader is challenged and encouraged to read each one with an introspective mind state. One should not have to ask themselves *what does this quote mean*? The question should be *what does this quote mean to ME*? Or, *how does this quote relate to someone or something I'm familiar with*? From the PerspectVe™ of these last two questions, real introspection and learning can occur not only from what I (the author) meant by it, but also what it means to you.

I have spent hundreds of hours researching the wording and structure of my quotes and philosophies for originality but within this piece of work, you will not find any references from authors, doctors, or venerable professors. In its physical form, what you are holding is a book. However this is not just a book, it is a body of art…a *creation* of new ideas from the mind and empirical observations of LIFE. Put on your spiritual thinking caps and leave the scientific hats alone for a while.

I pray that you enjoy this read and my goal is that you get *IT*!...*Improved Thinking* that is…

LIFE Philosophies

1. If you are in a do or die situation, it's better to focus on the doing than the dying.

2. **Keep dropping jewels on the people who need them. Eventually they may find themselves inside of a treasure chest.**

3. God doesn't FORCE his/her words on anybody; and I won't PRESSURE you to believe what I say. But I worry about what it's going to take to MAKE you listen.

4. **Even a quality woman cannot change a man...but when she tells him her expectations she can rewire his brain to the point where...he will change himself.**

5. Before you are a professional, you are a person. Great professionals combine their professionalism with their personality, because even in the word *professional*, one can spell the words PERSON and LIFE.

6. **The world will either be blessed or burdened by your presence. Decide your journey and choose wisely.**

7. Life is like the jury in a courtroom. It's not about what the TRUTH is or who's right or wrong. It's simply about figuring out which CASE makes the most sense to YOU.

8. **It's going to cost a lot of money to make your DREAMS come true. It's going to cost you your LIFE to live SOMEONE ELSE'S dream.**

9. Find symbolic meaning in every area of your life.

10. **B.L.A.C.K - Brave Leaders And Courageous Kings.**

11. Sometimes we mistake certain qualities in our family and friends as being potential, when it's not really potential. The mistake comes because we want them to be who WE want them to be, instead of us being comfortable with THEIR DECISION to be who they are.

12. **Life is like a house for sale…no matter how nice we look, or how much we think we're worth, people are still going to compare us to the environment we are in and the people and things around us.**

13. Don't accept people telling you that you forgot where you came from because they may be the same people who have forgotten where they've wanted to go.

14. **If someone else can do it, it doesn't mean that you can do it. It just means that it can be done. You have to figure out if YOU can do it.**

15. One of the best things you can give someone is SIMPLY the encouragement to get whatever it is that they want...themselves.

16. **LIFE is Living In Fascinating Experiences.**

17. Pay attention to what you do when you're bored because it could be what's blocking your success.

18. **There are more people living their dream than we think because some people have BAD DREAMS. They wake up in horror, and that's exactly what they are living in...HORROR.**

19. Many people choose not to live their dreams due to the fear of suffering through the nightmares. It's these same people who are usually unaware that they're already LIVING the NIGHTMARE and KILLING the DREAM.

20. **There will be long days, long nights, and long weeks. But life is short, so take advantage of the time that is LONG.**

21. Life is like a hotel room; people get a wakeup call and go right back to sleep.

22. **People may give you a reason to do something, but no one can make you do anything you don't want to do. We need to understand the maladaptive nature of placing blame, and adapt towards taking responsibility to THINK and make smarter decisions.**

23. The more calm you are, the more clear you think, the more clear you think, the better decisions you will make.

24. **Your body is always trying to talk to you. It's always trying to communicate with you and tell you what's going on in the here and NOW for what may lay ahead. Remember that your MIND is the EAR to your BODY.**

25. Anyone can make you have an orgasm, but no one makes you orgasm like the person you are IN LOVE WITH.

26. **People tell you to take a leap of faith but are shocked when you actually do it because to the untrained mind, the beginning behaviors of greatness look a lot like insanity.**

27. If you're not where you want to be in life, you probably have an idea of where you're currently at in life. And this is the perfect place to be at in terms of recognizing where you want TO GO.

28. **You should be able to have better imaginary sex fantasizing about the person you are in love with than actually having sex with someone you are not in love with.**

29. Sex is within love. Love is not within sex.

30. **Some people have fallen in love with their *curses* and have unconsciously developed a hatred for their *gifts*.**

31. When you are able to recognize the spirit of God communicating INSIDE OF YOU, you have reached a higher spiritual frequency of life.

32. **Before you become the change that you *want* to see, you must first become the change you *NEED TO BE*.**

33. God speaks sign language. Most people just don't understand the signs.

34. **Do not allow others to make you feel guilty about being paid to use your talents and gifts because those are the same people who get paid NOT to use their talents and gifts.**

35. Sometimes people will offer you less than what you have as if it's more than what you've got.

36. **People want what they don't need and don't need what they want.**

37. Chase your passion, don't let your passion chase you.

38. **Change is like a one person road trip in a small car. There's only enough room for you and a few of your belongings; and most likely you are going to leave a lot of people and things BEHIND.**

39. People want to teleport to success instead of realizing the JOURNEY is the only way to get there.

40. **Ask yourself sometimes, *Who am I?* And don't worry too much about the answer. WORRY if you don't have an answer.**

41. One of the ways God speaks to you is through GREAT IDEAS.

42. **I don't FEEL that I'm special, but I believe that I'm special. Most people have it backwards, they feel that they are special, but they don't BELIEVE IT.**

43. CLEAN up your act, before you MESS up your life.

44. **Having a life with no purpose is like having a present that you don't want. Most people never find its use, won't use it, or will just throw it away.**

45. If you kill someone with kindness, someone still ends up DEAD. Maybe you should just let them LIVE with your kindness.

46. **People who want to change the world single-HANDedly are selfish. *Who asked or told you to change it?* These types of people don't realize that**

when it comes to change, everyone has a HAND in it.

47. Sometimes you may enter another person's dream. But remember, it's not necessarily YOUR DREAM.

48. **In a relationship, there's a difference between feeling like you want to leave versus needing to get away for a moment. Wanting to leave shows that the person is DONE and no longer interested. Needing to get away for a moment shows that <u>you are still committed</u>.**

49. If your life was ever TAKEN from you, what would the world be able to say was GIVEN from you?

50. **Success is whatever you think it is, but it isn't always** *what you think it is*.

51. When you're really good at something, you need to be sure about it and confident in it, because people will try to prevent you from becoming great at it.

52. **In the ways that people are different I am the same. In the ways that people are the same I am different.**

53. Freedom may cost a lot of money, but it can also pay a lot of money.

54. **Don't let prejudice or racism stop your success. You are not the representation of someone else's negative thoughts.**

55. Leadership is one of the powers of a super hero.

56. **If you are spending more energy trying to hold on to the money that you do have, you may not be focusing enough on retrieving the money that you could have.**

57. The moment you realize who you are, and you decide to be that person, the world around you will change. People will then see you for WHO YOU ARE instead of WHAT YOU WERE.

58. **God, I don't just thank you for LIFE, I thank you for the IDEA of me.**

59. There are no secrets to success. Successful people have always told us what we should and should not do. The problem comes in that WE DON'T LIKE DOING WHAT WE ARE TOLD.

60. **You can have whatever you want in a heartbeat. I just hope that your heart doesn't stop beating before you realize it.**

61. Sometimes the people providing help to people are the ones in need of the exact same help THE MOST.

62. **A part of the solution is recognizing our own contribution to the problem.**

63. When you choose to be hard headed, God will suit up some angels and send them your way to battle you. The goal is not to hurt you. The goal is to prevent you from hurting yourself.

64. **Many people hate their job with a passion and unfortunately that's the only passion that they have.**

65. Your *I don't want to's* are probably your *I need to's*.

66. **One cannot prove that greatness is inside of all of us. Technically, we don't know what's inside of other people. It's like a BRAIN. Scientists do not know everything that is inside of the brain. However, we do know that everyone has one. But in order to discern the real capability of someone's brain, it**

must be used. So cultivate your greatness and then we'll know that it is inside of YOU.

67. Many people have someone or something they would DIE for but there are few people who can tell you anything about what they would LIVE for.

68. **Be careful what you read because <u>what is written</u> isn't always *what it was*, because *what it was* isn't always <u>what is written</u>.**

69. If you do what others won't do, you can become what others won't be.

70. **If you are afraid to be wrong, you may never give yourself the chance to be right.**

71. Part of recognizing *who you are* is recognizing *who you are NOT*.

72. **Many times when we do what is bad for us - it feels good, and when we do what is good for us - it feels bad. The trick is to do more of what's good for us because it will feel GREAT. Decide how you want to feel.**

73. There are times in life when the wrath of God and Satan are very similar. The *difference* comes in that Satan's purpose is to destroy you and God's purpose is to DEVELOP you.

74. **If you are not willing to pay the price of success, don't desire the life of success.**

75. A conversation amongst a group of intelligent people with NO self control is not much different than a conversation amongst fools.

76. **It is difficult to hear the whispers of God when you are bombarded with the noisiness of man.**

77. Do not limit your financial goals just because they say *the more money the more problems*. That does not mean that the less money you have the LESS PROBLEMS you will have.

78. **Make your dream world your real world.**

79. Saying someone is like-minded does not mean that they are EXACTLY LIKE YOU.

80. **If you are not willing to pay the price of CRIME, do not desire a life of crime.**

81. Too often too many people desire birthday gifts and holiday gifts instead of having the desire to open up their God-given gifts.

82. **Your body is the ear to your mind and your mind is the other ear to your body.**

83. Be aware that they best way to create a slave is to never let the person know that they are a slave.

84. **Family is like a garden of flowers. You all grow together; some of you will blossom and some won't. But the difference is that unlike the flowers, the family –most likely, will not die together. So it's better to enjoy the growth that HAS happened before the death that WILL HAPPEN.**

85. Everyone wants to ask you how you became successful instead of recognizing what you were doing when you were becoming successful.

86. **There is no plan that a man can create to destroy another man's life. But when a man accepts a plan that he has not created for HIS OWN life, he has already been destroyed.**

87. Pray for yourself and others to be blessed beyond your own/their own healthiest and happiest imaginations and dreams as well as your own/their own most wise and intelligent capabilities, while bringing great healthy glory to God.

88. **If you want to see what hell is like just allow your negative thoughts about yourself to become your way of life.**

89. Find spiritual meaning in every area of your life.

90. **Every torch gets passed but every torch doesn't have a bright flame.**

91. You are not defined by your pay stub. Make a living, but don't let your living make you.

92. **If money is the root of all evil, the human mind is the seed.**

93. There are many people in college who are there to get a DEGREE but do not want to learn. Meanwhile, there are a lot of people who want to learn but cannot find the time or afford to go to college.

94. **Little learning is done when you try to learn EVERYTHING. More learning is done when you begin figuring out and learning what interest you.**

95. You will never FIND out how to make money if you are constantly afraid to LOSE it.

96. **So many people are caught up in the chaos of what THEY HAVE TO DO at their job that they do not realize what their job HAS DONE TO THEM.**

97. Do not get your wants met and leave your needs wanting.

98. **We don't need more grants, donations, or playgrounds to make the world a better place. We need more people to make a serious decision to dedicate themselves to become better.**

99. When the mind is in a good place it will create a good place. Therefore in order to make the world a better place, you need to put your mind in a better place.

100. **People in your success circle will challenge you to travel into your areas of difficulty and SUCCEED there.**

101. Success doesn't have to be something that you come from, but it doesn't have to be something that you run from.

102. **In counseling psychology we say** *hurt people hurt people***. But rarely do we explore if** *healed people heal people***. If so, we need to explore the psychological definition of what it means to be healed.**

103. People want to see you FAIL and it may very well happen. But the difference between YOU and THEM is that you turn failure into SUCCESS and they have turned failure into a LIFESTYLE.

104. **A woman may look up to a man's vision but a man must live up to the vision.**

105. Rich thinking won't do you any good if you have a poor mind.

106. **If you get a chance to talk...SPEAK. If you get a chance to speak...SAY SOMETHING. And if you get a chance to say something...GIVE THEM AN EXPERIENCE THAT THEY WON'T FORGET!**

107. As an entrepreneur, I don't fear being told no because I have faith in being told YES!

108. **You may have a certain responsibility** *in* **someone else's life but you are not responsible** *for* **someone else's life. They are responsible for that.**

109. Greatness is not taught. It is desired, acted upon, and made into a lifestyle.

110. **When you are able to listen to the world spiritually, you are able to listen to the world literally.**

111. Some of the best help you will ever receive is receiving no help at all.

112. **There are people in the present who are more committed to their past than they are their future.**

113. If RESPONSIBILITY or ACCOUNTABILITY had a favorite holiday it would be Halloween because they scare a lot of people.

114. **People manage to graduate from high school, college, their masters and/or doctoral programs, but few people manage to graduate from their pain, problems and trauma.**

115. If you are focused on the stress, you are missing the chance to be blessed.

116. **I wouldn't hurt a fly as long as that fly doesn't try to hurt ME.**

117. If you want to stand out in life stop standing in the same place.

118. **Being the golden child is old news to a platinum person.**

119. There will be people who have more than you who will be jealous of you even though you have less than them. The reason is because you have EVERYTHING it takes to exceed them.

120. **Sometimes people will dislike you before you even become successful simply because you've CHOSEN to do what it takes to be successful.**

121. If you don't make your stress work for you it will work against you.

122. **Love is like a paycheck, by the time you receive it a lot of it has already been taken away. Then you give away so much of what's left to other people that there's not enough left for YOURSELF.**

123. Some people are so upset about what they are not getting from the world that it inhibits them from focusing on what they need to be giving to the world.

124. **Treat stress like your employee and make it work FOR YOU.**

125. Everyone is a work in progress. The problem comes when you stop seeing progress in your work.

126. **50 cent was shot nine times and did not DIE because of the 10th shot. God gave him *another shot* to try again at life.**

127. Love is hard to find because many people have a built in GPS that leads them directly to pain and grief.

128. **The goal should not be to get people out of the streets. The goal should be to get 'the streets' out of people.**

129. Don't look for a job to take care of you. Look for opportunities to take of yourself. That's entrepreneurship.

130. **Many times, your purpose in life is found through your pain.**

131. How can you be *the chosen one* if you have not chosen to be comfortable with who you are?

132. **It is just as easy to catch a spiritual sickness from someone as it is to catch a cold from someone.**

133. Life is the reward to complete your purpose. If you refuse to complete your purpose then your life is made difficult or taken away.

134. **It is hard to become better if you're not around better people.**

135. When you talk to millionaires/billionaires about what they did to get wealthy, the conversation really isn't that *deep*. It's not what they say that amazes you; it's what they DON'T SAY that amazes you because most likely what they DO SAY –you have heard before. There is no real secret. The fact is…they have simple practices and beliefs and they just do what most people refuse to do.

136. **Why should we have to be the first one to admit when we're wrong but the last one to say anything when we are right?**

137. Sometimes insanity is doing what is normal and saneness is doing what is uncommon.

138. **Do not place your goals and dreams in the abilities of other people. If those abilities ever DEBILITATE…so do your dreams.**

139. Some of us find life to be difficult because we have holy thoughts but demonic tendencies.

140. **Though the Diagnostic and Statistical Manual (DSM) is used in a clinical sense, it can also be used in Decoding Spiritual Matters (DSM).**

141. When you find the *present* in the *process* of your *pain*, you will find the *gifts* that *God* has for you to *gain*.

142. **A great education will you make a living. A great business will make you a fortune.**

143. People will call you cheap because you won't buy them the things they refuse to buy or can't afford to buy themselves.

144. **Many times the family and friends of an entrepreneur expect to receive products and services for free. Those same family members and friends don't realize that the expectation to receive something for free in life, will COST them.**

145. Your job is not necessarily your life, but your life IS your job.

146. **A big part of therapy is dealing with the content of what you brought in (the past), what you bring in (the present), and creating a bridge-of-meaning towards where you want to go.**

147. The problems we go through in life are the wrapping paper God wraps *the gift* in.

148. **Intelligence is not knowing the answer, intelligence is figuring out the answer.**

149. Knowledge is not knowing the answer, knowledge is being aware of the information.

150. **Laziness is a drug that breaks down and kills the mind and spirit.**

151. People resist *the cure* but insist on *the pain*.

152. **Even if we don't judge a book by its cover, we must still recognize the cover the author chose to go with.**

153. Don't be a master of someone else's life if you're an amateur within your own.

154. **Most people will never have the money they could have because they're too worried about losing the money they do have.**

155. Be careful what you do because what you do is doing something to you.

156. **If you are carrying around dead weight you should stop giving it LIFE...** *it's dead.*

157. Respect is a two-way street not an alleyway.

158. **Many people are living double lives. They live the dream in their sleep and they live the nightmare when they wake up.**

159. People desire what they are not willing to work for and are not willing to work for what they desire.

160. **If who you are isn't worth more than what you've got then what you've got isn't worth much at all.**

161. If you wouldn't go to the extreme for it, don't dream for it.

162. **Who you are can hold you back from what you could be.**

163. Make the best of what you've got or else what you don't have will get the best of YOU.

164. **Sometimes money and success is like bad sex. There's more fun in the lead up of what you thought it was going to be than** *actually having it*.

165. Your ideal life-partner should be like a TSA; someone who is willing to work with your baggage.

166. **Some people have to be treated like routing numbers; you have to keep them** *in-check*!

167. The best you that you can give somebody else is just that…the BEST YOU.

168. **As an entrepreneur one must understand that many times people have money even when they say they don't. What they don't have is a good enough reason** *from you* **as to why they should give you their money.**

169. It's bad enough to see people being victimized against their own will. It's worse to see someone using their own will to victimize themselves.

170. **People who say that all men cheat are unconsciously creating an unwritten rule that it's acceptable.**

171. Stress is <u>S</u>ituational <u>T</u>raining <u>R</u>egiments <u>E</u>xperienced – <u>S</u>ophisticating <u>S</u>elf.

172. **Sometimes we don't realize that the basket we are putting all our eggs in has a hole at the bottom.**

173. People say that time is money. Therefore, if you don't put any time into your craft, don't expect to put too much money into your bank account.

174. Sometimes, the first thing we should do in a situation is the last thing we do and the last thing we should do is the first thing that we do.

175. Life is like a tattoo because it will scar you; but the real beauty comes in the meaning that you create for it.

176. I'd rather be wise with little intelligence than intelligent with little wisdom.

177. No work ethic + No Action = Future Jealousy
Successful People

178. Why keep asking the same question if the only answer you want is the answer you already have in your mind?

179. Efficacy doesn't come in what you KNOW, it comes in what you can DO.

180. A good P-L-A-N is not *planning life as needed.* **A good plan is to see the "*n*"-result and** *plan life ahead.*

181. If you are running from hard work, you are running straight into a hard life.

182. Some people choose NOT to create their own life. Instead, they choose a life that is created FOR THEM.

183. People go out of their way to be around another person's greatness but do little to bring the greatness out of themselves.

184. Sometimes people mistake Gods tests for us as the devils torture.

185. It's better to open the door and let God in so He/She doesn't have to break the door down and break in.

186. **Success is like a barter system. It wants something in exchange from you.**

187. Problems should not define your life. You should define the problems IN your life for the benefit OF your life.

188. **Don't wait for a long term challenge in life that forces you to make a long term change in life.**

189. Even though God is trustworthy, it is hard to trust God when we can't trust ourselves.

190. **Reading or listening to something once does not guarantee you** *understood* **or** *heard* **everything that time.**

191. Much of who we are comes from what we were taught. The possibility of who we could be comes in what we were not taught.

192. **I'd rather die failing on a mission to succeed than to die succeeding on a mission to fail.**

193. A purpose with passion, ambition, and determination does not allow for boredom.

194. **Sometime people get to the end of their life and realize that it was like a** parking lot **during the** holiday season**. They entered and saw that it was so jam-packed that they just settled for a spot far away from** *where they wanted to go***. Only to find out that there was a spot that would have got them closer to what they** *CAME TO DO***.**

195. Financial freedom should not be granted before spiritual, mental, and emotional development. Regardless of the amount of money you have, if you don't have these three things you will never be FREE.

196. **The relationships with the people** you know **have contributed to what** you have. **The lack of relationships with the people** you don't know **may be contributing to what** you don't have.

197. Some of the most peaceful and trustworthy people in the world carry guns and some of the most corrupt and dangerous people in the world carry bibles.

198. **Live your dreams or die living your nightmare.**

199. God usually doesn't give you a choice of how you die but God does give you the option to choose how you live.

200. **Living my purpose is my drug of choice.**

201. Some people are so accustomed to going without the things they say they want, that when they are offered it -they say they don't want it.

202. **Boredom is God's gift to those people who need extra time to figure out their purpose.**

203. People go out of their way to be around greatness but do little to bring the greatness out of themselves.

204. **Time is the humans attempt to measure existence.**

205. Don't believe in God WHEN you need to; believe in God BECAUSE you need to.

206. **If you are going through some tough times and someone asks you how you're doing, tell them you have had better experiences but you have never seen a day better than today.**

207. If you want to END up with EVERYTHING do not be afraid to START over with NOTHING.

208. **The fear of wealth induces the maladaptive idea that there is safety in poverty.**

209. Poor people don't understand the power of personal development. That is why they're poor. Rich and wealthy people do understand the power of personal development. That is why they're rich and wealthy.

210. **God presents situations for us to have opportunities to work on choice-development.**

211. God will REMOVE you from something in order to REMAKE you into something.

212. **Poor people aren't poor because of what they *don't have*. Poor people are poor because of what they *don't know*.**

213. Oppressed people have to deal with situations when their inner voice says *'I shouldn't do this/that because of who I am'*. The oppressor's inner voice says *'I have the FREEDOM to do this/that because of who I am'*.

214. **Calmness is the birth place of clarity.**

215. As men, some of us can be so accustomed to meeting women who allow us to lust them that when we meet a woman who has a standard that requires us to love them, we don't know what to do.

216. **Sometimes your side hustle should be your main hustle and your main hustle shouldn't be your hustle at all.**

217. *Cool people* invest in the short term things in life. Great people invest in the long term things in life.

218. **Don't blame *the culture* for the belief systems that you took from it. Blame yourself for the belief systems that you took from the culture.**

219. If you can control your emotions you can control your life.

220. **No book or materials of such likeness can report the exact truth because** *the truth* **is only present for a specific time in <u>existence</u>. What these books and things do is explore and interpret the** *experience* **of THE TRUTH.**

221. All of us are only a second or an experience away from a life changing event; but how we choose to experience life can change how we experience events.

222. **When God gives you an opportunity to grow – don't shrink!**

223. Many of the problems children have began before they were even born or conceived. The parents were making bad decisions when they were kids and their poor decision making continued into adulthood. The cycle of problems just perpetuates.

224. **If you put your future in someone else's future you will always be stuck in the past.**

225. People should be able to buy *your service* but they should NEVER be able to *buy you*!

226. **Most people have never M.E.T.T themselves. They are blind to the <u>M</u>essages surrounding them, they don't understand the information their <u>E</u>motions are trying to give them, they rarely challenge their <u>T</u>houghts, and they don't pay attention to the <u>T</u>hemes in different areas of their lives.**

227. Our physical bodies are costumes put over our spiritual bodies. The real spelling of these costumes is c-o-s-t-t-o-m-b-s. Because the price (the cost) to wear them, is our life (the tomb).

228. **Part of figuring out** *who you are* **is figuring out** *who you are not.*

229. People enter the year saying Happy New Year but they end the year no happier than they were entering it.

230. **Emotional intelligence is the glue that holds a relationship together.**

231. Many kids believe that because adults tell them that they are smart and have potential, their future success is guaranteed. Smarts and potential do not guarantee anything.

232. **The mind is a selfish being; because what the mind wants, the body doesn't always need. And what the body needs, the mind doesn't always want…Keep in mind what the body needs, the mind should need to.**

233. Having the facts does not necessarily mean having the truth. Facts are simply accepted concepts that are agreed upon by the masses. *The truth* can be something totally different.

234. **Strength without power is called** <u>stress</u>. **When you are simply** *strong* **you become the dumping ground for the baggage of other people because they know you're strong enough to take it. But when you're** *powerful***, people respect your boundaries more and they find other people to dump their baggage on…leaving you with** *less stress.*

235. There are two *i's* and no *u's* in *opinion.* That should tell you something about the opinions of other people.

236. **A great idea is the <u>I</u>ndividual <u>D</u>ream <u>E</u>nergetically** *Actualized.*

237. The 5 O's of success are recognizing an <u>O</u>pening in the market, which then leads to a new <u>O</u>pportunity.

From here, you must increase your Output within your *plan of action.* This output must be Ongoing. And when these things take place, you will increase your Outcomes.

238. Life is like a building; each level creates a new story.

239. Confidence without character is arrogance.

240. The first three letters within the word PRIDE are RIP and the last three letters are DIE. And this is because *pride kills* **whoever it is** *within.*

241. Humans make family a blood connection. God makes family a spiritual connection.

242. If you refuse to listen then you refuse to be listened to.

243. A parent does not develop a child into a leader by giving the child orders and directives. Doing so will surely result in the development of a follower. A parent must expose the child to the behaviors of a leader, or more importantly, model the behaviors themselves, discuss the qualities of a leader with the child, and provide opportunities for the child to exercise and apply leadership skills. In this, the child gets to experience a leader and the experience of being the leader.

244. The four W's of success is the idea that successful people WORK. They *W*isely *O*btain *R*esearched *K*nowledge. **They don't WAIT. They don't** *W*aste *A*nd *I*gnore *T*ime. **They understand WEALTH. They are aware that** *W*ishing *E*liminates *A*ction – *L*eading *T*o *H*eartbreak (or *H*avoc). **And finally, successful people know how to WIN. They know how to** *W*ork *I*n *N*umbers.

Boxing Philosophies in LIFE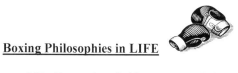

245. Do not be afraid to use your POWER.

246. Do not let your competition OUTWORK you.

247. If you don't use your POWER, you will FALL victim to someone else's POWER.

248. Even if someone is victorious in FIGHTING your BATTLE, it still ends up being your LOSS and their WIN.

249. You will have UPS and DOWNS but don't ever COUNT yourself OUT. Make every SECOND count!

250. ROLL with the PUNCHES, but COUNTER BACK.

251. VICTORY requires preparation and TRAINING.

252. People will JUDGE you but it does not mean they will be RIGHT!

253. Success takes a COMBINATION of things.

254. Find a way around people and things BLOCKING your success.

255. If you don't take action, your opportunity can SLIP away.

256. Having CONFIDENCE eliminates fear.

257. You can only RUN from problems so long before they TIRE you out.

258. **Don't beat yourself up about the bad things going on in your life. Focus on dealing with the situation that's trying to BEAT YOU UP!**

259. Be able to PROTECT YOURSELF at all times but do not be so GUARDED to the point where you begin to HURT yourself.

260. **It takes COURAGE to step into an environment where you know you can be HURT…Remember that life is like an EXERCISE. When it starts HURTING and BURNING, that means it is working. However, you'll never know it if you don't PUSH through it.**

261. There will be times when you will need to STRETCH yourself beyond what you think you can do.

262. **Only REST when you need to, not when <u>you want to</u> because rest can be addicting, and the MINUTE YOU REST may turn into the minute you GIVE UP!**

263. Don't be too FAST to jump on things in LIFE, but don't be too SLOW to act on opportunities when they come.

264. **Success involves EXTENDING yourself and FOLLOWING THROUGH with things.**

265. Find your BALANCE in life or suffer the *downfall* of being OFF BALANCE.

266. **Whatever you are AIMING to do in life, you must focus on the things you are TARGETING.**

267. In life you will have to keep some people at a DISTANCE.

268. **In life, there will be times when you have to start at the BOTTOM and WORK your way to the TOP.**

269. No matter where you are at in life, do what WINNERS do and get a COACH!

270. **You should know who is really in YOUR CORNER because there may be some people who are only there to PROMOTE themselves.**

271. Have good head movement, because an idle mind is an easy TARGET.

272. **Turn your stress into your STRENGTH and your problems into your POWER.**

273. No PAIN, no gain. No stress, no success.

274. **Put yourself in a POSITION of POWER.**

275. Don't HOLD on to knowledge…HIT people with what you know.

276. **Get HOOKED on success!**

277. In LIFE when someone is COUNTING on you that's one thing. In BOXING when someone is counting on you that can lead to a KO. Be careful who you're counting on and who is counting on you!

278. **Outsmart the OPPOSITION.**

279. People try to GO AGAINST God and that will always be a LOSING BATTLE.

280. **Unsafe sex is a lot like professional boxing. When you are not WEARING PROTECTION, you are increasing the risk of damaging your health. And sometimes the DAMAGE can be LONG-LASTING.**

281. There are people who are blessed with TALENT and people who *cursed* with talent.

282. **Rarely is someone cursed with SKILL because skill is not *put in you*, it is developed by you.**

283. STUDY yourself in order to get better because there may be someone studying you!

284. **No one is born a CHAMPION, you must earn that TITLE.**

285. In LIFE it will be difficult to get THE RESULTS you want if you are not ACTIVE enough in your endeavors.

286. **Finding a job is like boxing because you've got to look for OPENINGS.**

287. You should not have to do too much PUSHING PEOPLE away if you make them RESPECT your boundaries.

288. **In order to *change* or to succeed, you do not always have to make major changes in your life. Sometimes all you have to do is make minor ADJUSTMENTS within what you're already doing.**

289. At some point your business may TAKE A HIT so it's good to have PROTECTION.

290. **Don't just TAP into your success; STEP into it.**

291. In LIFE, if the JABS people throw at you are not dangerous or harmful, it can be better to just CATCH them and let them ROLL OFF YOUR SHOULDER because it takes too much ENERGY to get out of the way or COUNTER back.

292. When you take a HIT and you learn how to RECOVER, you uncover layers of yourself and see what YOU ARE REALLY MADE OF.

293. Some people SET THEMSELVES UP to be HURT, and when they get hurt they act surprised and take no accountability in having any contribution to their own PAIN.

294. Your greatness will make you a TARGET but that should not stop you from TARGETING your greatness.

295. Life is like the three minute rounds in boxing…you only have a certain amount of TIME to do whatever it is that you CAME TO DO.

296. Don't allow people to TRAP you in a situation that you can't get out of.

297. Sometimes we celebrate before things happen and what happens is that the real celebration doesn't happen.

298. People *succeed* **in criticizing you for the rewards you've gotten out of life but** *fail to see* **all the WORK you have PUT IN to your life.**

299. Becoming limited in your ABILITIES to function in what you're *passionate for* does not mean becoming limited to function in what you're *passionate about*! It may simply mean that you must find a different function…And in this process you may be surprised to find *something new that you are passionate for*.

300. People are not WINNERS because things go their way. They are winners because of how they go about things.

I thank you for reading! You can reach me at www.PerspectVe.com. Remember to spell the word PerspectVe without the "i" because to broaden your own horizons, sometimes you have to take yourself out of your own PerspectVe. Take care and I pray you a happy, healthy, and meaningful life of success through God.

Made in the USA
Middletown, DE
23 October 2024